The Gods of Kemet

An Afrocentric Perspective

by

Ayanna Newman

Grosvenor House
Publishing Limited

All rights reserved
Copyright © Ayanna Newman, 2020

The right of Ayanna Newman to be identified as the author of this work has been asserted in accordance with Section 78 of the Copyright, Designs and Patents Act 1988

The book cover is copyright to Ayanna Newman

This book is published by
Grosvenor House Publishing Ltd
Link House
140 The Broadway, Tolworth, Surrey, KT6 7HT.
www.grosvenorhousepublishing.co.uk

This book is sold subject to the conditions that it shall not, by way of trade or otherwise, be lent, resold, hired out or otherwise circulated without the author's or publisher's prior consent in any form of binding or cover other than that in which it is published and without a similar condition including this condition being imposed on the subsequent purchaser.

A CIP record for this book
is available from the British Library

ISBN 978-1-83975-425-8

Contents

Images:
Front cover: Pharaoh Djoser
Back Cover: Djed Pillar

In pursuit of the Khasekhemwy votives

Pantheon of the Gods

OGDOAD OF KHMUNU (City of Eight representing primordial elements of creation)

Nu/Naunet (Mehet-Weret) — Amun/Amunet — Heh/Hauhet — Kek/Kauket
(Water) Nun — (Invisibility) (formerly adopted as creator god 12th Dynasty) — (Infinity) — (Darkness)

Amun/Amunet
consort
Mut/Bastet (lioness)
issue
Khonsu (god of moon)

↓
PRINCIPAL LIST
↓
created
ATUM - - - - - - - - - consort Iusaaset (siblings) - - - - - - - - - - Khnum - - - - - - - - - Neith
(creator god)
1st image in human form.
↓
children
Shu + Tefnut (lioness)
↓
created
Geb/Seb + Nut
(god of earth) (sky goddess)
↓
parents of
Osiris — Set — Nephthys
(God of Dead)
consort – Isis (health, wisdom, marriage)
↓
children
Anubis (embalming and dead) - - - - - - - children
Wepwawet + Anput
(opener of the way)
Min (fertility)
Horus (light)
(embodiment of Kemetic kingship and protector eye)
↓
Ihy - (music and joy produced by the sistrum)
(child of Horus and Hathor)

Set
↓
killed Osiris, fought with Horus to be ruler of the living
↓
prevailed assisted by Thoth
(god of wisdom)

Khnum
↓ Harsephes (aspect of)
↓ Khepri (aspect of) - - - - - siblings Atum + Ra
↓
(head of ram and associated with water)
consort
Satet, Heqet, Menhit, Nebtu
↓
children
Anuket, Serket, Ra, Thoth

Thoth ↓ (consort Ma'at)
Ra ↓
(consort Hathor)
issue
Sekhmet - - - - - - - - - - with Ptah - - - - - - - - - - - - - - - - - linked to Imhotep] deified vizier to Pharaoh Djoser (3rd Dynasty)
(lioness) (creator god of craftsmen and architects)
↓
2 sons
- [Maahes - he who is true beside her (lion)
- [Nefertum - healing, fragrance, incense and beauty

Narrative

The history of ancient Kemet/Egypt is divided into three main periods: the Old Kingdom (about 2,700 - 2,200 BC), the Middle Kingdom (2,050 - 1,800 BC), and the New Kingdom (1,550 - 1,100 BC). The New Kingdom was followed by a period called the Late New Kingdom, which lasted to about 343 BC. (Intermediate kingdoms - those without strong ruling families - filled the gaps of time in between the Old, Middle, and New Kingdoms). Additionally, hints to primevalism exist in the was-sceptre, symbol of authority of male gods.

Central to this history are the gods Osiris and Isis.

The history of Kemet, barring the discovery of new major dynasties, spans 34 dynasties, which include immediately preceding the run into Christianity (and, after the 31st Dynasty or second period of Persian rule); the Kings of Macedon 332 - 305 BC, the Ptolemies (Greece) 305 - 30 BC and the Roman Emperors 30BC - 305 AD, which Roman Empire went on to conquer England, having prior to that created the concepts of Serapis (a mix of the gods Osiris and Apis) and Horus (the child), both images eventually to represent Jesus within Kemet/Egypt and worldwide. The Roman Empire (43AD) brought the belief system of Christianity to England (whose devotional systems were still in the stage of rudimentary and sparsely documented paganism). Christianity in the guise of Roman Catholicism was installed in England which was eventually replaced by Henry VIII with the Church of England/Anglicanism - (monotheism).

There are concepts in the world that are not always immediately perceptible and constantly evolving with every new discovery, for instance, such as the ancient Kemet belief in concepts of invisibility, darkness and infinity - how they as first peoples viewed/ negotiated these concepts and applied them within their daily lives; together with other African life sciences and disciplines developed and recorded in Kemetic culture; so, hence naming the gods to reflect experience of their environment. As we have been socialized through history with a Eurocentric analysis of African history i.e. a Kemetic/Egyptian history that is not part of the African continent; evidence of first civilizations and discoveries attributable to them have been homogenized to a predominantly Eurocentric view. So too, experimentation and innovation disregarded i.e. Pepy I (6th Dynasty) use of copper in place of stone as medium for statues.

The principal chart/list of gods and supplementary lists, are produced and constructed as a start to acclimatize to the language of Kemet and the relationship of the gods to each other; and to assist to examine the question of spirituality of Kingship (and spirituality generally) within ancient Kemet.

The gods, both principal and minor/supplementary as represented in various stages or points in Kemet's history can be recorded in forms that are not hieroglyph/medu neter but invariably in human personification. The chart of the principal gods and their relationship to each other - to include evidence of Amun (who existed throughout the earliest history of Kemet but was formally adopted as creator god in place of Atum in the 12th Dynasty under the rule of Pharaoh Amenemhat I); shows a polytheistic system in existence prior to 3rd Dynasty Kemet which houses individuals such as Ptah, Pharaoh Djoser/Netjerikhet and Imhotep (vizier to Djoser and novitiate of Ptah). Ptah joined the pantheon as a creator god. Pharaoh Djoser's vizier Imhotep represented an earthly existence which eventually became deified; not uncommon within ancient Kemet, i.e. as later with Hardedef son of Pharaoh Khufu of 4th Dynasty (who commissioned the Pyramids at Giza) or Amenhotep, son of Hapu, scribe and architect under Amenhotep III of 18th Dynasty.

The supplementary lists of gods contain gods that can be associated throughout the history of Kemet with the principal deities or gods that may only be associated individually with any of the 42 nomes of Kemet.

The Pharaohs themselves were also deemed to be gods.

This well documented and complex polytheist society created in Kemet prevailed throughout 31 Dynasties of ancient Kemet and its physical evidence survives to date to continue to take its place in history, despite attempts at cultural appropriation and subsumption by Greek, Roman and subsequently other elements of modern day culture.

OGDOAD OF KHMUNU

(City of Eight representing primordial elements of creation)

God/Goddess	***Role***
Amun	a creator god, patron deity of the city of Thebes (centre of worship for Amun); and the preeminent deity of Kemet during the New Kingdom/onset of 12th Dynasty (1991 BC). Representing invisibility.
Amunet	female counterpart of Amun.
Heh	personification of infinity.
Hauhet	female counterpart of Heh.
Kek	god of chaos and darkness, as well as being the concept of primordial darkness.
Kauket	female counterpart of Kek.
Nu	personification of the formless, watery disorder from which the world emerged at creation.
Naunet	female counterpart of Nu.

Ennead - Council of Nine

(Creators of the world and Tribunal presiding the Osiris Myth)

God/Goddess	***Role***
Atum	a creator god and solar deity (Atum Ra), first god of the Ennead.
Geb	an earth god (associated with earthquakes).
Isis	wife of Osiris and mother of Horus, linked with funerary rites, motherhood, protection and magic. [She became a major deity in Greek and Roman religion as the mother of Jesus].
Nephthys	consort/sister of Set, who mourned Osiris alongside Isis.
Nut	a sky goddess.
Osiris	god of death and resurrection who rules the underworld and enlivens vegetation, the sun god (at night), and deceased souls.
Set	god of violence and chaos banished to the desert. Murderer of Osiris and enemy of Horus.
Shu	embodiment of wind and air.
Tefnut	goddess of moisture.

Hieroglyph/Medu Neter

Principal List

God/Goddess	Role
Anput	goddess of the dead and mummification.
Anubis	god of embalming and protector of the dead.
Anuket	goddess of Kemet's southern frontier regions, particularly the lower cataracts of the Nile.
Atum	a creator god and solar deity (Atum Ra), first god of the Ennead.
Bastet	goddess represented as a cat or lioness, linked with protection from evil.
Geb	an earth god (associated with earthquakes).
Harsephes/Heryshef	a ram god associated with water and Khnum.
Hathor	one of the most important goddesses, linked with the sky, sexuality and motherhood, music and dance, foreign lands and goods, and the afterlife. One of the many forms of the Eye of Ra.
Heket/Heqet	frog goddess said to protect women in childbirth.

God/Goddess	***Role***
Horus	a major god, usually shown as a falcon or as a human child, linked with the sky, the sun, kingship, protection and healing. Often said to be the son of Osiris and Isis.
Ihy	a child deity born to Horus and Hathor, representing the music and joy produced by the sistrum.
Imhotep	novitiate of Ptah, vizier to Pharaoh Djoser (3rd Dynasty).
Isis	wife of Osiris and mother of Horus, linked with funerary rites, motherhood, protection and magic. [She became a major deity in Greek and Roman religion as the mother of Jesus].
Iusaaset	female counterpart of Atum, grandmother of the gods.
Khepri	a solar creator god, often treated as the morning form of Ra and represented as the scarab beetle. Associated with Khnum.
Khnum	a ram god, the patron deity of Elephantine, who was said to control the Nile flood and give life to gods and humans.
Khonsu	a moon god, son of Amun and Mut or Bastet.
Maahes	a lion god, son of Ptah and Sekhmet/Bastet - he who is true beside her. Often mistaken for Sekhmet particularly when in the guise of Min.

God/Goddess	***Role***
Ma'at	goddess who personifies truth, justice and order; and 42 principles of order governing daily living in Kemet.
Mehet-Weret	a celestial cow goddess associated with Nu, gave birth to Ra.
Menhit	a lioness Nubian war goddess.
Min	god of virility/fertility.
Mut	consort of Amun.
Nebtu	deity of the desert oasis and a wife of Khnum.
Nefertum	god of the lotus blossom who emerged from the primeval waters and a god of perfume and aromatherapy.
Neith	a creator and hunter goddess, sister of Atum and Khnum.
Nephthys	consort/sister of Set, who mourned Osiris alongside Isis.
Nut	a sky goddess.
Osiris	god of death and resurrection who rules the underworld and enlivens vegetation, the sun god (at night), and deceased souls.

God/Goddess	***Role***
Ptah	a creator deity and god of craftsmen.
Ra	the foremost Kemetic sun god, involved in creation and afterlife.
Satet	consort of Khnum, goddess of Kemet southern frontier regions.
Sekhmet	a lioness goddess, said to be both destructive and violent and capable of warding off disease, protector of the Pharaohs who led them in war, the consort of Ptah and one of the many forms of the Eye of Ra.
Serket	a scorpion goddess, invoked for healing and protection.
Set	god of violence and chaos banished to the desert. Murderer of Osiris and enemy of Horus.
Shu	embodiment of wind and air.
Tefnut	goddess of moisture.
Thoth/Djehuty	a moon god, and a god of wisdom, writing and scribes.
Wepwawet	a jackal god (the opener of the way), connected with afterlife.

Supplementary List A

God/Goddess	*Role*
Aker	god of the earth and the horizon.
Ammit	goddess who devoured condemned souls.
Amenhotep, son of Hapu	a scribe and architect in the Court of Pharaoh Amenhotep III (18th Dynasty), later deified for his wisdom.
Am-heh	a dangerous underworld god, linked to Ammit, god of divine retribution.
Anat	war and fertility goddess.
Anhur/Onuris	god of war and hunting.
Anti	falcon god, ferryman for greater gods.
Apedemak	a warlike lion god from Lower Nubia.
Apep	a serpent deity, personification of malevolent chaos and said to fight Ra in the underworld every night.

God/Goddess	***Role***
Apis	a live bull worshipped as god and seen as the manifestation of Ptah.
Arensnuphis	deity of Lower Nubia.
Ash	god of Libyan desert and oases west of Kemet.
Astarte	a warrior goddess from Syria.
Aten	sun disk deity, became the focus of monotheistic Atenist belief under the reign of Pharaoh Akhenaten (18th Dynasty).
Baal	sky and storm god from Syria.
Ba'alat Gebal	a Canaanite goddess, patroness of Byblos, adopted into Kemetic religion.
Babi	a baboon god characterized by sexuality and devourer of entrails.
Banebdejedet	a four-headed ram god, patron of city of Mendes.
Ba-Pef	a little-known underworld deity.
Bat	cow goddess from early Kemet, eventually adsorbed by Hathor.

God/Goddess	***Role***
Bennu	a solar and creator deity, depicted as a bird.
Bes	apotropaic god, represented as a dwarf, particularly important in protecting children and women in childbirth.
Buchis	a live bull, a manifestation of Montu.
Dedun	a Nubian god said to provide Kemet with incense and other resources that came from Nubia.
Ha	god of Libyan desert and oases west of Kemet.
Hapi	personification of the Nile flood.
Hatmehit	fish goddess worshipped at Mendes.
Hedetet	a minor scorpion goddess.
Heka	personification of magic.
Hesat	a maternal cow goddess.

God/Goddess	***Role***
[Horus (the child)	Harpocrates in Greek culture c. Alexander the Great, a construct that would eventually morph into the image of the infant Jesus. This god was created along with Serapis with a view to unifying the belief systems in Kemet and to invoke silence].
Hu	personification of the authority of the spoken word.
Iah	a moon god.
Iat	a goddess of milk and nursing.
Imentet	an afterlife goddess closely linked with Isis and Hathor.
[Ishtar	Semitic warrior goddess occasionally mentioned in Kemetic text].
Kherty	a underworld god, usually depicted as a ram.
Mafdet	protector goddess against snakes and scorpions and guardian of the chamber of Pharaoh.
Mandulis	a Lower Nubian deity.
Mehit	a lioness god consort of Anhur.

God/Goddess	***Role***
Matit	a funerary cat goddess.
Mehen	a serpent god who protects the barque of Ra as it travels through the underworld.
Meretseger	a cobra goddess, in charge of guarding and protecting Thebes.
Meskhenet	a goddess who presided over childbirth.
Mnevis	a live bull worshipped as a manifestation of Ra.
Montu	god of war and the sun.
Nebethetepet	a female counterpart to Atum.
Nehebu-Kau	a protective serpent god.
Nehmetawy	a minor goddess, consort of Nehebu-Kau or Thoth.
Nekhbet	a vulture goddess of Upper Egypt.
Neper	god of grain.

God/Goddess	*Role*
Nepit	goddess of grain and counterpart of Neper.
Pakhet	a lioness goddess worshipped around Beni Hasan (cemetery site).
Qetesh	a goddess of sexuality from Syria and Canaan adopted into Kemet religion.
Raet-Tawy	a female counterpart to Ra.
Renenutet	an agricultural goddess.
Reshep	a Syrian war god adopted into Kemet religion.
Renpet	a goddess who personified the year.
Seker	a god of the afterlife.
[Serapis	a Greco-Egyptian god from the Ptolemaic Period who fused traits of Osiris and Apis with those of several other Greek gods. Said to be husband of Isis who, like her was adopted into Greek and Roman religion within and outside Kemet].
Seshat	goddess of writing and record keeping, depicted as a scribe.

God/Goddess	***Role***
Shai	personification of fate.
Shed	a god believed to save people from danger and misfortune.
Shesmetet	a lioness goddess, aspect of Bastet or Sekhmet.
Shezmu	a god of wine and oil presses who also slaughters condemned souls.
Sia	personification of perception and thoughtfulness.
Sobek	crocodile god, representing strength and power.
Sopdu	god of sky of Kemet eastern border regions.
Sopdet	deification of the star Sirius.
Ta-Bitjet	a minor scorpion goddess absorbed into Isis.
Tatenen	personification of the first mound of earth to emerge from chaos in ancient Kemet creation myths.
Taweret	hippopotamus goddess, protector of women in childbirth.

God/Goddess	***Role***
Tenenet	goddess of beer and brewing, also present at childbirth.
[Tutu	a protective god from Greco- Roman era].
Unut	a goddess represented as a snake or a hare.
Wadjet	a cobra goddess of Lower Egypt.
Wadj-wer	personification of Mediterranean Sea or lake of the Nile Delta.
Weneg	a son of Ra who maintains cosmic order.
Werethekau	a goddess (human-headed Cobra) who protects the Pharaoh.
Wosret	a minor goddess of Thebes.
Yam	a Syrian god of the sea who appears in some Kemetic text.

Supplementary List B

God/Goddess	***Role***
Aken	associated solely with Book of Dead and the underworld.
Amenet	afterlife goddess, daughter of Horus and Hathor.
Anta	an aspect of Mut, worshipped at Tanis and consort of Amun.
Andjety	fertility god associated with Busiris, eventually absorbed into Osiris.
Auf	an aspect of Ra.
Beset	female aspect of Bes.
Cavern Deities	nameless gods who lived in caverns, referred to in Egyptian Book of the Dead.
Celestial Ferryman	boatman who ferried justified dead in the afterlife.
Denwen	serpent and dragon god.
Fetket	servant of Ra.

God/Goddess	***Role***
Field of Offerings	region in the afterlife devoted to Osiris.
Field of Reeds	paradise in afterlife where justified souls admitted to.
Forty -Two Judges	deities who presided with Osiris in judgement of the soul in the afterlife.
Four Sons of Horus	canopic jar protector gods – Duamutef, Hapy, Imsety and Qebehsenuef.
Gengen-Wer	goose god, force of creative energy.
Hardedef	son of Pharaoh Khufu (4th Dynasty) deified for wisdom.
Hathor-Nebet-Hetepet	worshipped at Heliopolis, associated with Ra.
Haurun	associated with Giza Sphinx.
Heset	goddess of food and drink and beer.
Heret Kau	goddess of the Old Kingdom, later absorbed by Isis.
Hetepes-Sekhus	personification of the eye of Ra.

God/Goddess	***Role***
Horus the Elder	born of Geb and Nut, brother of Osiris.
Iabet	fertility goddess absorbed by Isis.
Ipy	hippopotamus mother goddess.
[Isis-Etheria	Greek version of Isis].
Iw	creation goddess with qualities of Hathor and Nebet-Hetepet.
[Jupiter-Amun	Roman god].
Kabechet	daughter of Anubis.
Kagemni	vizier of Pharaoh Sneferu (4th Dynasty), deified and worshipped as a god of wisdom.
Khentekhai	4th Dynasty crocodile god later absorbed by Horus.
Khentiamenti	fertility god absorbed by Osiris.
Lady of the Acacia	grandmother of the gods see: Iusaaset.

God/Goddess	***Role***
Lady of the Sycamore	see: Hathor.
Lake of Flowers (Lily Lake)	body of water in afterlife souls of justified dead crossed to reach paradise.
Lates-Fish	Nile perch sacred to the goddess Neith.
Mau	cat deity, aspect of Ra.
Mekhit	Nubian goddess of war.
Merit	goddess of music.
Mestjet	lion headed goddess, aspect of Ra.
Nekheny	falcon god eventually absorbed by Horus.
[Panebtawy-Horus	see: Harpocrates/Horus the child].
Pataikos	amuletic god of the power of Ptah.
Peak	personification of highest point of cliffs.

God/Goddess	***Role***
Peteese and Pihor	brothers who drowned in the Nile, associated with Osiris.
Ptah-hotep	scholar deified for Wisdom Text.
Ptah-Sokar-Osiris	hybrid god of three, worshipped during Middle Kingdom.
Raettawy	female aspect of Ra.
Ra-Harakhte	falcon god, amalgam of Ra and Horus representing sunrise and sunset.
Reret	hippopotamus protective deity.
Ruty	twin lion gods representing east and west horizons.
Sah	astral god.
Sebiumeker	procreation and fertility deity in Meroe, Kush.
Sed	5th Dynasty jackal deity absorbed into Wepwawet.
Sepa	centipede protective god.

God/Goddess	***Role***
Seret	5th Dynasty protector lion goddess in a region of Kemet inhabited by Libyans.
Shentayet	protective widow goddess associated with Isis.
Shepet	crocodile headed goddess associated with Reret and Taweret.
Sky bull	presided over heaven and afterlife and was seen as husband to seven cows that are seen with him.
Sothis	personification of the Sirius Star which appearance heralded the annual inundation of the Nile.
[Sutekh	Semitic name for Set].
[Tasenetnofret	said to be the mother of Panebtawy].
Tayet (Tait)	weaver goddess of the garments of the Pharaoh including bandages on mummification.
Tetrads	representing completeness and balance.
Tjenenyet	12th Dynasty consort of Montu.

God/Goddess	***Role***
Tree Goddesses	notably Isis, Hathor, and Nut.
Tutu	worshipped toward latter part of Kemetic history to ward off evil.
Uat-Ur	personification of Mediterranean Sea.
Wenenu	aspect of Osiris or Ra, consort of Unut.
Wepset	protective goddess, destroys enemies of Osiris.
Zenenet	alternative name for Isis.

Hieroglyph/Medu Neter

Pharaohs of Kemet

[list partially attributable to Khaemwaset son of Ramses II (19th Dynasty)]

The Old Kingdom

First Dynasty (c. 3100 - 2890) BC

Narmer	Aha	Djer	Djet	Den	Adjib	Semerkhet	Qaa

Second Dynasty (c. 2890 - 2686) BC

Hetepsekhemwy	Nebra	Ninetjer	Peribsen	Sekhemib	Khasekhemwy

Third Dynasty (c. 2686 - 2613) BC

Netjerikhet/Djoser	Sekhemkhet	Sanakht

Fourth Dynasty (c. 2613 - 2494) BC

Sneferu	Khufu	Djedefra	Khafra	Menkaura	Shepseskaf

Fifth Dynasty (c. 2494 - 2345) BC

Userkaf	Sahura	Kakai	Ini	Kaiu	Isesi	Unas

Sixth Dynasty (c. 2345 - 2181) BC

Teti	Pepy I	Nemtyemsaf	Pepy II

Seventh Dynasty (c. 2181) BC

No Pharaohs of note but marked as end of Old Kingdom.

The Middle Kingdom

Eighth Dynasty (c. 2181 - 2130) BC

Wadjkara | Demedjibtawy | Qakara Iby

Ninth and Tenth Dynasties (c. 2130 - 2040) BC

Khety | Merykara

Eleventh Dynasty (c. 2130 - 1991) BC

Sehertawy Intef | Wahankh Intef | Nakhtnebtepnefer Intef | Nebhepetra/Mentuhotep

Sankhkara/Mentuhotep | Nebtawyra/Mentuhotep

Twelfth Dynasty (c. 1991 - 1786) BC

Amenemhat I | Senusret I | Amenemhat II | Senusret II | Senusret III | Amenemhat III

Amenemhat IV | Sobekneferu

Thirteenth Dynasty (c. 1786 - 1674) BC

Wegaf | Ameny Intef Amenemhat | Hor | Amenemhat Sobekhotep | Khendjer | Sobekhotep

Khasekhembra | Neferhotep | Sihathor | Sobekhotep | Ay | Iykhernofret Neferhotep

Fourteenth Dynasty (c. 1700 - 1674) BC

Nehesy

Fifteenth Dynasty (c. 1674 - 1567) BC

Khyan | Apepi

Sixteenth Dynasty (c. 1674 - 1567) BC

Anather | Yakobaam

Seventeenth Dynasty (c. 1674 - 1567) BC

Intef | Sobekemsaf | Taa(qen) | Kamose

The New Kingdom

Eighteenth Dynasty (c. 1567 - 1320)

Ahmose I | Amenhotep I | Thutmose I | Thutmose II | Hatshepsut [Queen] | Thutmose III

Amenhotep II | Thutmose IV | Amenhotep III | Akhenaten | Smenkhkara | Tutankhamun

Ay | Horemheb

Nineteenth Dynasty (c. 1320 - 1200) BC

Ramses I | Sety I | Ramses II | Merneptah | Sety II | Amenmesse | Siptah

Tausret [Queen]

Twentieth Dynasty (c. 1200 - 1085) BC

Setnakht | Ramses III | Ramses IV | Ramses VI | Ramses IX | Ramses XI | Herihor

The Late New Kingdom

Twenty-First Dynasty (c. 1085 - 945) BC

Nasbanebdjed | Pasebakhaenniut I | Amenemopet | Saimon | Pasebakhaenniut II | Pinudjem | Menkheperra

Twenty-Second Dynasty (c. 945 - 715) BC

Sheshonq I | Osorkon I | Sheshonq II | Osorkon II | Takelot II | Shehonq III | Pamiy | Horsiese

Twenty-Third Dynasty (c. 818 - 715) BC

Padibastet | Input | Nimlot | Peftjauabastet

Twenty-Fourth Dynasty (c. 727 - 715) BC

Tefnakht | Bakenrenef

Twenty-Fifth Dynasty (c. 747 - 656) BC

Pi(ankh)i | Shabako | Shabitko | Taharqo | Tanutamani

Kushite Rulers

Aspelta | Harsiotef | Amanislo | Natakamani

Twenty-Sixth Dynasty (c. 664 - 525) BC

Psamtek I | Nekau | Psamtek II | Wahibra | Ahmose II | Psamtek III

Twenty-Seventh Dynasty *or first Persian Period* (c. 525 - 404) BC

Cambyses | Darius I | Xerxes I | Artaxerxes I | Padibastet | Inaros

Twenty-Eighth Dynasty (c. 401 - 399) BC

Amyrtaeus

Twenty-Ninth Dynasty (c. 399 - 380) BC

Nefaarud I | Hakor

Thirtieth Dynasty (c. 380 - 343) BC

Nectanebo I | Djedhor | Nectanebo II

Thirty-First Dynasty *or second Persian Period* (c. 343 - 332) BC

Darius III

Kings of Macedon (c. 332 - 305) BC

Alexander the Great | Phillip Arrhidaeus | Alexander IV

The Ptolemies/Greek Rule (305 - 50) BC

Ptolemy I | Ptolemy II | Ptolemy III | Ptolemy IV | Ptolemy V | Ptolemy VI | Ptolemy XII

Ptolemy XV | Cleopatra VII [Queen]

Rebel Kings against Ptolemies: Horwennefer | Ankhwennefer

Roman Emperors (3BC - AD 305)

Kaisaros/Augustus	Tiberius	Domitian	Trajanus	Diocletian

***Dynastic dates vary slightly between historians*

www.ingramcontent.com/pod-product-compliance
Lightning Source LLC
LaVergne TN
LVHW080020110826
845148LV00019B/1170
9781839754258